DAILY
GRATITUDE

JANUARY 17

All serious daring
starts from within.

~ EUDORA WELTY

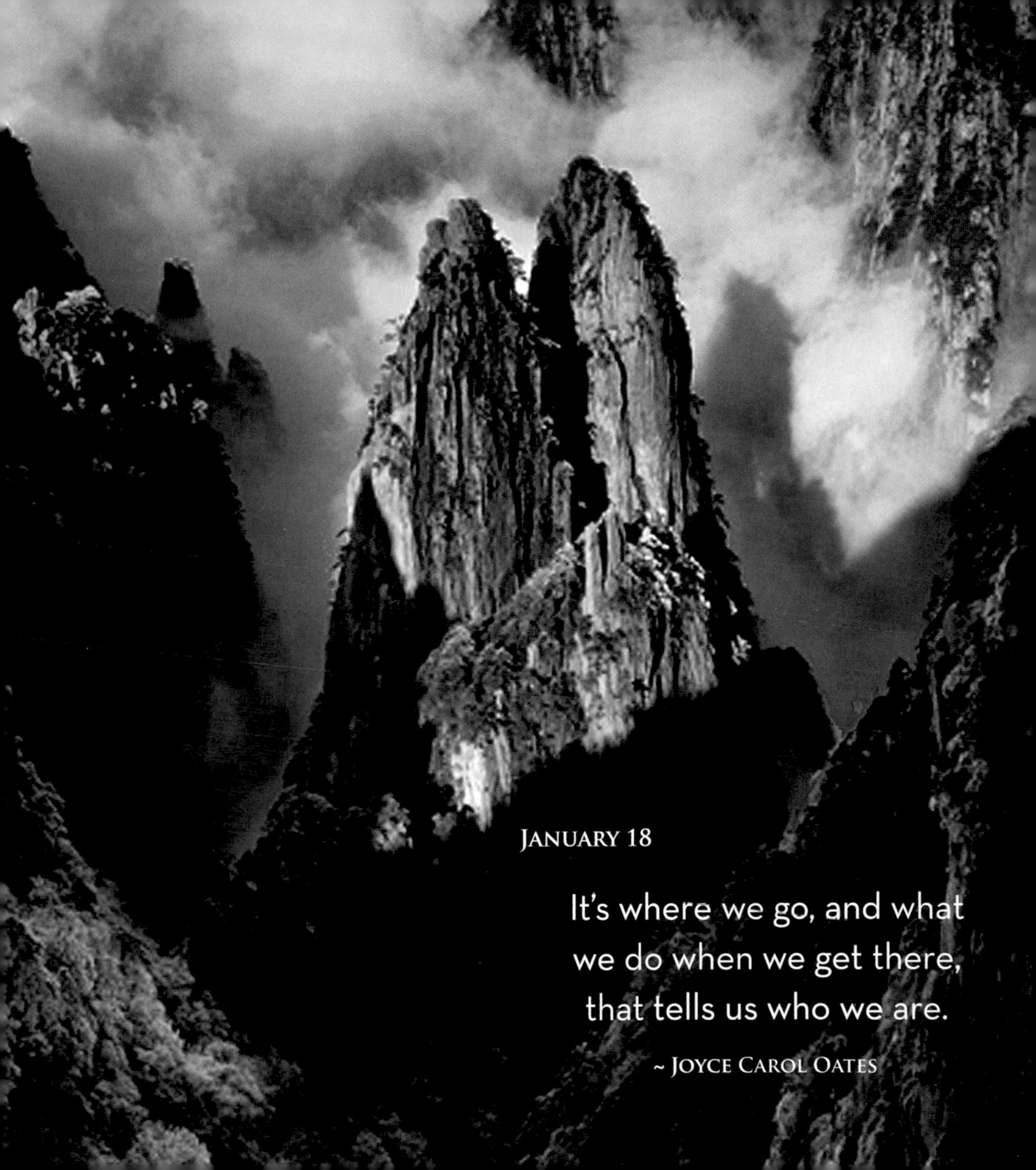

JANUARY 18

It's where we go, and what
we do when we get there,
that tells us who we are.

~ JOYCE CAROL OATES

The secret of joy in work is contained
in one word—excellence. To know how
to do something well is to enjoy it.

~ PEARL S. BUCK

Love and work are the
cornerstones of our humanness.

~ SIGMUND FREUD

JANUARY 21

Between the
wish and the thing the
world lies waiting.

~ CORMAC MCCARTHY
ALL THE PRETTY HORSES

The very least you can do in your life
is figure out what you hope for. And the most
you can do is live inside that hope, running down
its hallways, touching the walls on both sides.

~ BARBARA KINGSOLVER
ANIMAL DREAMS

JANUARY 23

For us there is only the trying.

~ T. S. ELIOT

JANUARY 24

Life loves to be taken by
the lapel and told:
I'm with you kid, let's go.

~ MAYA ANGELOU

Far away there in the sunshine
are my highest aspirations.
I may not reach them, but I can look
up and see their beauty, believe in
them, and try to follow them.

~ LOUISA MAY ALCOTT

You can't cling to the side your whole life. One lesson every parent needs to teach a child is, "If you don't want to sink, you better figure out how to swim."

~ Jeannette Walls

The world of the future is in our making.
Tomorrow is now.

~ ELEANOR ROOSEVELT

Remember to look up at the stars
and not down at your feet.
Try to make sense of what you see
and wonder about what makes the
universe exist. Be curious.

~ STEPHEN HAWKING

JANUARY 29

The more one does
and sees and feels, the
more one is able to do.

~ AMELIA EARHART

Ultimately, we know deeply that
the other side of every fear is freedom.

~ MARILYN FERGUSON
THE AQUARIAN CONSPIRACY

There is a great deal of
unmapped country within us.

~ GEORGE ELIOT
DANIEL DERONDA

February

FAMILY

Remember we all stumble, every
one of us. That's why it's a comfort
to go hand in hand.

~ EMILY KIMBROUGH

Families are ecosystems.
Each life grows in response
to the lives around it.

~ MARY SCHMICH

The soul is healed by
being with children.

~ FYODOR DOSTOYEVSKY

FEBRUARY 4

Having a child is surely the
most beautifully irrational act that
two people in love can commit.

~ BILL COSBY

Other things may change us, but
we start and end with the family.

~ ANTHONY BRANDT

Mother is the home
we come from.
She is nature, soil, ocean.

~ ERICH FROMM

FEBRUARY 7

God could not be everywhere,
and therefore he made mothers.

~ JEWISH SAYING

The family is one of
nature's masterpieces.

~ GEORGE SANTAYANA

Give a little love to a child,
and you get a great deal back.

~ JOHN RUSKIN

What is a family, after all, except memories?
—haphazard and precious as the contents
of a catchall drawer in the kitchen.

~ JOYCE CAROL OATES
WE WERE THE MULVANEYS

Call it a clan,
call it a tribe, call it a
family. Whatever you
call it, whoever you
are, you need one.

~ JANE HOWARD

Family is not an important thing.
It's everything.

~ MICHAEL J. FOX

What can we make of the
inexpressible joy of children?
It is a kind of gratitude.

~ ANNIE DILLARD

Making a decision to have a child—it's momentous. It is to decide forever to have your heart go walking around outside your body.

~ ELIZABETH STONE

One thing I had learned from
watching chimpanzees with their infants
is that having a child should be fun.

~ JANE GOODALL

A sibling may be the keeper of one's identity,
the only person with the keys to one's
unfettered, more fundamental self.

~ MARIAN SANDMAIER

FEBRUARY 17

There is no way to be a
perfect mother, and a million
ways to be a good one.

~ JILL CHURCHILL

After a good dinner,
one can forgive anybody,
even one's own relations.

~ Oscar Wilde

Every child begins the world again.

~ HENRY DAVID THOREAU

There are two lasting bequests we
can give our children. One is roots.
The other is wings.

~ HODDING CARTER

A mother is a story with no beginning.
That is what defines her.

~ Meghan O'Rourke

FEBRUARY 22

For there is no friend like a sister,
in calm or stormy weather.

~ CHRISTINA ROSSETTI

FEBRUARY 23

To us, family means putting
your arms around each
other and being there.

~ BARBARA BUSH

Sticking with your family is
what *makes* it a family.

~ MITCH ALBOM

We must take care
of our families
wherever we find them.

~ ELIZABETH GILBERT

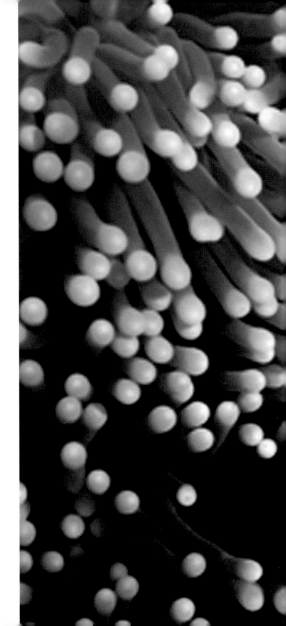

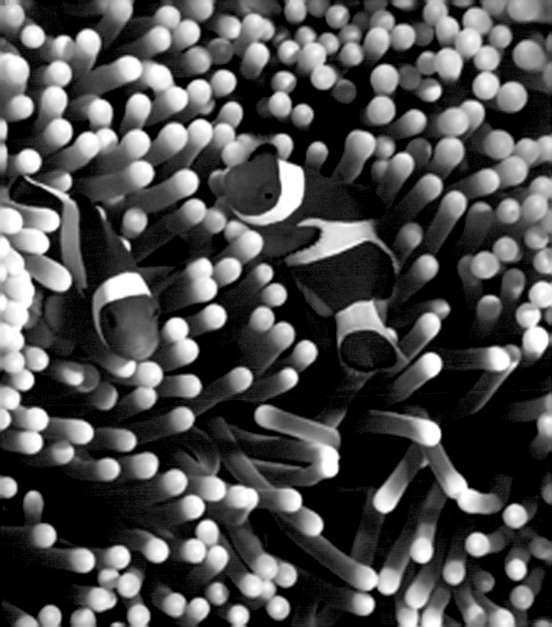

You don't choose your family. They are
God's gift to you, as you are to them.

~ DESMOND TUTU

I believe the choice to
become a mother is the choice
to become one of the greatest
spiritual teachers there is.

~ OPRAH WINFREY

Always kiss your children goodnight—
even if they're already asleep.

~ H. JACKSON BROWN, JR.

MARCH

FRIENDSHIP

Good friends, good books and a
sleepy conscience: this is the ideal life.

~ MARK TWAIN

MARCH 2

You meet your friend,
Your face brightens—you have struck gold.

~ KASSIA

MARCH 3

What a delight it is to make friends
with someone you have despised!

~ COLETTE

Some people need a red carpet rolled
out in front of them in order to walk
forward into friendship. They can't see the
tiny outstretched hands all around them,
everywhere, like leaves on trees.

~ MIRANDA JULY

Best friend, my
well-spring in
the wilderness!

~ GEORGE ELIOT

It's the friends you can call up
at 4 A.M. that matter.

~ MARLENE DIETRICH

The process of falling in love at first sight
is as final as it is swift in such a case,
but the growth of true friendship
may be a lifelong affair.

~ SARAH ORNE JEWETT
THE COUNTRY OF THE POINTED FIRS

A true friend is someone
who thinks that you are a good
egg even though he knows that
you are slightly cracked.

~ BERNARD MELTZER

The typical expression of opening
Friendship would be something like,
"What! You too?
I thought I was the only one."

~ C. S. LEWIS

We secure our friends not by
accepting favors, but by doing them.

~ THUCYDIDES

We learned how to create beauty where none
exists, how to be generous beyond our means,
how to change a small corner of the world—
just by making a little dinner for a few friends.

~ GABRIELLE HAMILTON

When I count my blessings,
I count you twice.

~ IRISH PROVERB

Love is like the wild-rose
briar, Friendship like
the holly-tree—The holly is
dark when the rose-briar
blooms, But which will
bloom most constantly?

~ EMILY BRONTË

MARCH 14

Ah, how good it feels!
The hand of an old friend.

~ HENRY WADSWORTH LONGFELLOW

Laughter is the shortest
distance between two people.

~ VICTOR BORGE

Wishing to be friends
is quick work,
but friendship is a
slow-ripening fruit.

~ ARISTOTLE

My friends have made
the story of my life.

~ HELEN KELLER

Friendship is
a sheltering tree.

~ SAMUEL TAYLOR
COLERIDGE

MARCH 19

There's no word yet for old
friends who've just met.

~ JIM HENSON

Friendship is the only cement that
will hold the world together.

~ WOODROW WILSON

Each friend represents a world in us,
a world possibly not born until
they arrive, and it is only by this meeting
that a new world is born.

~ ANAÏS NIN

Friendship often ends in love;
but love in friendship—never.

~ CHARLES CALEB COLTON

"Why did you do all this for me?" he asked.
"I don't deserve it. I've never done anything for you."
"You have been my friend," replied Charlotte.
"That in itself is a tremendous thing."

~ E. B. WHITE
CHARLOTTE'S WEB

There is one friend in the life of each
of us who seems not a separate person,
however dear and beloved, but an expansion,
an interpretation, of one's self.

~ EDITH WHARTON

Friendship with one's self is all important,
because without it one cannot be
friends with anyone else in the world.

~ ELEANOR ROOSEVELT

Good friends are like
shock absorbers.
They help you take the
lumps and bumps
on the road of life.

~ FRANK TYGER

Sometimes our light goes out but is
blown into flame by another human being.
Each of us owes deepest thanks to those
who have rekindled this light.

~ ALBERT SCHWEITZER

Only your real friends will tell
you when your face is dirty.

~ SICILIAN PROVERB

We are all travelers in the
wilderness of this world, and
the best we can find in
our travels is an honest friend.

~ ROBERT LOUIS STEVENSON

I hope you don't mind that I put
down in words, how wonderful life
is while you're in the world.

~ BERNIE TAUPIN

You can make more friends in two months
by becoming interested in other people
than you can in two years by trying to get
other people interested in you.

~ DALE CARNEGIE

APRIL

LOVE

APRIL 1

Love should be allowed.
I'm all for it.

~ TRUMAN CAPOTE
BREAKFAST AT TIFFANY'S

APRIL 2

The sound of a kiss is not so loud
as that of a cannon, but its
echo lasts a great deal longer.

~ OLIVER WENDELL HOLMES, SR.

Never say love is like
anything—it isn't.

~ MICHAEL CHABON
THE MYSTERIES OF PITTSBURGH

APRIL 4

With love, you have to work out whether your roots have so entwined together that it is inconceivable that you should ever part. Because this is what love is. Love is not breathlessness.

~ LOUIS DE BERNIÈRES
CAPTAIN CORELLI'S MANDOLIN

The trout enjoys the river,
The whale enjoys the sea,
And dogs love most an old lamp-post,
But you're my cup of tea.

~ W. H. AUDEN

A happy marriage is
a long conversation which
always seems too short.

~ ANDRÉ MAUROIS

The story of human intimacy is one
of constantly allowing ourselves to see
those we love most deeply in a new, more
fractured light. Look hard. Risk that.

~ CHERYL STRAYED

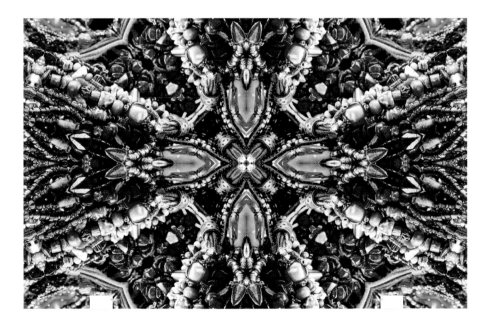

My bounty is as boundless as the sea,
My love as deep; the more I give to thee,
The more I have, for both are infinite.

~ WILLIAM SHAKESPEARE
ROMEO AND JULIET

It's no trick loving somebody at their best.
Love is loving them at their worst.

~ TOM STOPPARD
THE REAL THING

If you had really loved
something, wouldn't a little
bit of it always linger?

~ SUSAN ORLEAN
THE ORCHID THIEF

Love is everything it's cracked up to be.
It really is worth fighting for, being brave for,
risking everything for. And the trouble is, if you
don't risk everything, you risk even more.

~ ERICA JONG

APRIL 12

If ever two were one, then surely we.
If ever man were loved by wife, then thee.

~ ANNE BRADSTREET

He never wanted to
be away from her.
She had the spark of life.

~ ALICE MUNRO
AWAY FROM HER

Love is the true means by
which the world is enjoyed:
our Love to others
and others' Love to us.

~ THOMAS TRAHERNE

Sexiness wears thin after a while
and beauty fades, but to be married
to a man who makes you laugh every
day, ah, now that's a real treat.

~ JOANNE WOODWARD

A good marriage was one in
which each person thought he or
she was getting the better deal.

~ ANNE LAMOTT
JOE JONES

Ah, life grows lovely where you are.

~ MATHILDE BLIND

I love her and that's the beginning
and end of everything.

~ F. Scott Fitzgerald

APRIL 19

Lovers don't finally meet
somewhere. They're in each
other all along.

~ RUMI

Whatever our souls are made of,
his and mine are the same.

~ EMILY BRONTË
WUTHERING HEIGHTS

I have learned not to worry about love;
but to honor its coming with all my heart.

~ ALICE WALKER

Gratitude is a twofold love—
love coming to visit us and
love running out to
greet a welcome guest.

~ HENRY VAN DYKE

Our union is like this:
You feel cold, so I reach
for a blanket to cover our
shivering feet . . . You ache
with loneliness one night
so much you weep, and
I say here is a rope, tie it
around me, I will be your
companion for life.

~ HAFEZ

Nobody has ever measured,
not even poets, how much
the heart can hold.

~ ZELDA FITZGERALD

APRIL 25

Gratitude is a shortcut
which speedily leads to love.

~ THÉOPHILE GAUTIER

Love is or it ain't.
Thin love ain't love at all.

~ TONI MORRISON
Beloved

Where there is great love there
are always miracles.

~ WILLA CATHER

The things that we love
tell us what we are.

~ ST. THOMAS AQUINAS

He felt now that he was
not simply close to her,
but that he did not know where
he ended and she began.

~ Leo Tolstoy
Anna Karenina

APRIL 30

We can only learn
to love by loving.

~ IRIS MURDOCH

MAY

HAPPINESS

MAY 1

I stuck my head out the window
this morning and spring
kissed me bang in the face.

~ LANGSTON HUGHES

Happiness is equilibrium. Shift your weight.

~ Tom Stoppard

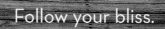

MAY 3

Follow your bliss.

~ JOSEPH CAMPBELL

Life is so endlessly delicious.

~ RUTH REICHL

MAY 5

Joy is the simplest
form of gratitude.

~ KARL BARTH

We can only be said to be alive
in those moments when our hearts
are conscious of our treasures.

~ THORNTON WILDER

Happiness often sneaks
in through a door you didn't
know you left open.

~ JOHN BARRYMORE

Happiness quite unshared
can scarcely be called
happiness; it has no taste.

~ CHARLOTTE BRONTË

It isn't the big pleasures that
count the most; it's making a great
deal out of the little ones.

~ JEAN WEBSTER

Happiness is anyone and anything
at all that's loved by you.

~ CLARK GESNER

MAY 11

They seemed to come suddenly
upon happiness as if they had surprised
a butterfly in the winter woods.

~ EDITH WHARTON

MAY 12

Happiness is a place
between too
much and too little.

~ FINNISH PROVERB

That is happiness; to be dissolved
into something complete and great.

~ WILLA CATHER
MY ÁNTONIA

MAY 14

Love the moment, and the
energy of that moment will spread
beyond all boundaries.

~ SISTER CORITA KENT

MAY 15

When spring came, even the
false spring, there were no problems
except where to be happiest.

~ ERNEST HEMINGWAY
A MOVEABLE FEAST

MAY 16

Let us uncork all our
bottled up happiness.

~ PABLO NERUDA

MAY 17

Happiness is like a butterfly which, when pursued, is always beyond our grasp, but, if you will sit down quietly, may alight upon you.

~ NATHANIEL HAWTHORNE

The best way to pay for a
lovely moment is to enjoy it.

~ RICHARD BACH

Life is precious as it is.
All the elements for your happiness are
already here. There is no need to
run, strive, search, or struggle. Just be.

–THICH NHAT HANH

MAY 20

To like many people
spontaneously and without effort
is perhaps the greatest of all
sources of personal happiness.

~ BERTRAND RUSSELL

All happiness depends
on a leisurely breakfast.

~ JOHN GUNTHER

MAY 22

The constant happiness is curiosity.

~ ALICE MUNRO

MAY 23

Nothing is worth more than this day.

~ JOHANN WOLFGANG VON GOETHE

Too much of a good thing
can be wonderful.

~ MAE WEST

MAY 25

Be happy, and a reason
will come along.

~ ROBERT BRAULT

The soul is here for
its own joy.

~ RUMI

Happiness is not the means
to any end. It is the end.
It is its own goal.
It is its own purpose.

~ AYN RAND

One of the secrets
of a happy life is
continuous small treats.

~ IRIS MURDOCH
THE SEA, THE SEA

The three grand essentials to happiness in life are something to do, something to love, and something to hope for.

~ JOSEPH ADDISON

MAY 30

Let us be grateful to the
people who make us happy;
they are the charming gardeners
who make our souls blossom.

~ MARCEL PROUST

Yesterday is but a dream, tomorrow
but a vision. But today well-lived makes
every yesterday a dream of happiness, and
every tomorrow a vision of hope.
Look well, therefore, to this day.

~ Sanskrit proverb

JUNE

BEAUTY

What a morning—fresh as if issued
to children on a beach.

~ VIRGINIA WOOLF

may my heart always be open to little
birds who are the secrets of living

~ E. E. CUMMINGS

Live in the sunshine,
swim the sea,
Drink the wild air's salubrity.

~ RALPH WALDO EMERSON

The essence of all beautiful art,
all great art, is gratitude.

~ FRIEDRICH NIETZSCHE

The earth is warmer when you laugh.

~ Samuel Beam

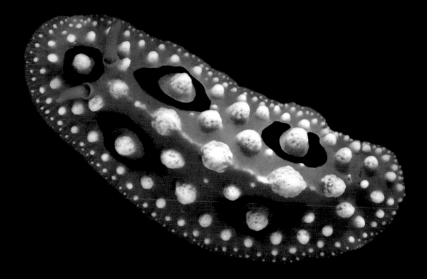

June 6

In all things of nature, there is
something of the marvelous.

~ Aristotle

Got no checkbooks, got no banks.
Still I'd like to express my thanks—
I got the sun in the mornin'
And the moon at night.

~ IRVING BERLIN

I'll tell you how
the Sun rose
A Ribbon at a time

~ EMILY DICKINSON

One cannot collect
all the beautiful shells
on the beach.
One can collect only
a few, and they are
more beautiful if they
are few.

~ ANNE MORROW LINDBERGH

Everything has its beauty,
but not everyone sees it.

~ CONFUCIUS

Nature seems to have implanted
gratitude in all living creatures.

~ SAMUEL JOHNSON

JUNE 12

Forget not that the earth delights
to feel your bare feet and the winds
long to play with your hair.

~ KAHLIL GIBRAN

JUNE 13

Set wide the window.
Let me drink the day.

~ EDITH WHARTON

There is a blessing in the air,
Which seems a sense of joy to yield
To the bare trees, and mountains bare,
And grass in the green field.

~ WILLIAM WORDSWORTH

JUNE 15

What makes a river so
restful to people is
that it doesn't have any
doubt—it is sure
to get where it is going,
and it doesn't want
to go anywhere else.

~ HAL BOYLE

JUNE 16

I believe in God,
only I spell it Nature.

~ FRANK LLOYD WRIGHT

So come, and slowly we will walk
through green gardens and marvel
at this strange and sweet world.

~ Sylvia Plath

Nobody sees a flower, really—it is so small—
we haven't time, and to see takes time,
like to have a friend takes time.

~ GEORGIA O'KEEFFE

Day's sweetest moments
are at dawn.

~ ELLA WHEFLER WILCOX

JUNE 20

Above all, watch with
glittering eyes the
whole world around
you because the
greatest secrets are
always hidden in the
most unlikely places.
Those who don't
believe in magic will
never find it.

~ ROALD DAHL
THE MINPINS

Let the rain sing you a lullaby.

~ LANGSTON HUGHES

The stars are like the trees in
the forest, alive and breathing.
And they're watching me.

~ Haruki Murakami

JUNE 23

Some people grumble that
roses have thorns; I am grateful
that thorns have roses.

~ ALPHONSE KARR

The poetry of earth is never dead.

~ JOHN KEATS

JUNE 25

Walk as if you are kissing
the Earth with your feet.

~ THICH NHAT HANH

Those who contemplate the beauty
of the earth find reserves of strength
that will endure as long as life lasts.

~ RACHEL CARSON

Going to the woods is going home.

~ JOHN MUIR

The littlest birds sing
the prettiest songs.

~ THE BE GOOD TANYAS

Even after all this time. The sun
never says to the earth, "You owe me."
Look what happens with a love like that.
It lights the whole sky.

~ HAFEZ

JUNE 30

At some point in life the world's beauty becomes enough. You don't need to photograph, paint or even remember it. It is enough.

~ TONI MORRISON
TAR BABY

JULY

ADVENTURE

Cease to inquire what the future
has in store, and to take as a
gift whatever the day brings forth.

~ HORACE

We all live in suspense,
from day to day, from hour
to hour; in other words, we are
the hero of our own story.

~ MARY MCCARTHY

If you want to conquer fear,
don't sit home and think about it.
Go out and get busy.

~ DALE CARNEGIE

There is a time for departure—even
when there's no certain place to go.

~ TENNESSEE WILLIAMS

If you come to a fork
in the road, take it!

~ YOGI BERRA

The road was new to me, as roads
always are going back.

~ SARAH ORNE JEWETT
THE COUNTRY OF THE POINTED FIRS

Dance till the stars come
down from the rafters! Dance,
dance, dance till you drop!

~ W. H. AUDEN

JULY 8

It's great to arrive,
but the trip's most always
most of the fun.

~ MALCOLM FORBES

The world is big and I want to have a
good look at it before it gets dark.

~ JOHN MUIR

There is no greater joy than to have an
endlessly changing horizon, for each day
to have a new and different sun.

~ CHRISTOPHER MCCANDLESS

No, no! The adventures
first, explanations take such
a dreadful time.

~ LEWIS CARROLL
ALICE'S ADVENTURES IN WONDERLAND

JULY 12

We love because it is
the only true adventure.

~ Nikki Giovanni

Cavort, dear, just cavort.

~ CAROL BURNETT

In summer, the song sings itself.

~ WILLIAM CARLOS WILLIAMS

Adventure is worthwhile in itself.

~ AMELIA EARHART

JULY 16

Only those who will risk going too far can
possibly find out how far one can go.

~ T. S. ELIOT

JULY 17

Have your adventures,
make your mistakes, and choose
your friends poorly—all these
make for great stories.

~ CHUCK PALAHNIUK

Let us decide on the route that
we wish to take to pass our life, and
attempt to sow that route with flowers.

~ Madame du Châtelet

It was the first peach
I had ever tasted.
I could hardly believe
how delicious.
At twenty-five
I was dumbfounded afresh
by my ignorance of the
simplest things.

~ TED HUGHES

We don't know who we are
until we see what we can do.

~ MARTHA GRIMES

JULY 21

Life itself is the
proper binge.

~ JULIA CHILD

July 22

If you obey all the rules,
you miss all the fun.

~ KATHARINE HEPBURN

To live is so startling, it leaves but little
room for other occupations.

~ EMILY DICKINSON

JULY 24

My favorite
thing is to go
where I've never
seen before.

~ DIANE ARBUS

JULY 25

When shall we live
if not now?

~ M. F. K. FISHER

All life is an experiment.
The more experiments
you make, the better.

~ RALPH WALDO EMERSON

Not all those who wander are lost.

~ J. R. R. TOLKIEN
THE FELLOWSHIP OF THE RING

JULY 28

Night is the other half of life,
and the better half.

~ JOHANN WOLFGANG VON GOETHE
WILHELM MEISTER'S APPRENTICESHIP

A journey is a person
in itself, no two are alike.

~ JOHN STEINBECK

Drink and dance and laugh and lie,
Love, the reeling midnight through,
For tomorrow we shall die!
(But, alas, we never do.)

~ DOROTHY PARKER

The biggest adventure
you can ever take is to live
the life of your dreams.

~ OPRAH WINFREY

AUGUST

HOME

Love begins at home.

–Mother Teresa

No one realizes how beautiful it is to travel until he comes home and rests his head on his old, familiar pillow.

~ LIN YUTANG

AUGUST 3

Be grateful for the
home you have, knowing
that at this moment,
all you have is all you need.

~ SARAH BAN BREATHNACH

Peace and a well-built house
cannot be bought too dearly.

–DANISH PROVERB

Home is the nicest word there is.

~ LAURA INGALLS WILDER

Where we love is home—
home that our feet may leave,
but not our hearts.

~ OLIVER WENDELL HOLMES, SR.

AUGUST 7

Home is a place not only of
strong affections, but of entire
unreserve; it is life's undress rehearsal,
its back-room, its dressing room.

~ HARRIET BEECHER STOWE

Home is a name, a word, it is a strong one;
stronger than magician ever spoke, or spirit
ever answered to, in the strongest conjuration.

~ CHARLES DICKENS
THE LIFE AND ADVENTURES OF MARTIN CHUZZLEWIT

Home is any four walls
that enclose the right person.

~ HELEN ROWLAND

There is no place more delightful
than one's own fireside.

~ CICERO

Stay, stay at home,
my heart and rest
Home-keeping hearts
are the happiest
For those that wander
they know not where
Are full of trouble
and full of care
To stay at home is best.

~ HENRY WADSWORTH LONGFELLOW

The ordinary acts we practice every day
at home are of more importance to
the soul than their simplicity might suggest.

–THOMAS MOORE

Home is the place where, when
you have to go there,
They have to take you in.

–ROBERT FROST

Traveling in the company of those
we love is home in motion.

~ LEIGH HUNT

The power of finding beauty
in the humblest things makes
home happy and life lovely.

~ LOUISA MAY ALCOTT
Jack and Jill: A Village Story

Wherever you are is my
home—my only home.

~ CHARLOTTE BRONTË
JANE EYRE

You can go other places, all right—you
can live on the other side of the world,
but you can't ever leave home.

~ SUE MONK KIDD
THE MERMAID CHAIR

Home is an invention on which
no one has yet improved.

~ ANN DOUGLAS

If light is in your heart,
you will find your way home.

~ RUMI

AUGUST 20

The ornament of a house is
the friends who frequent it.

~ RALPH WALDO EMERSON

Ah! There is nothing
like staying at home
for real comfort.

~ JANE AUSTEN
EMMA

We shape our dwellings, and
afterwards our dwellings shape us.

~ Winston Churchill

Home is wherever I'm with you.

~ EDWARD SHARPE
AND THE MAGNETIC ZEROS

The ache for home lives in all of us.
The safe place where we can go as
we are and not be questioned.

~ MAYA ANGELOU

There is nothing like returning
to a place that remains unchanged
to find the ways in which you
yourself have altered.

~ NELSON MANDELA

One's home is like a delicious piece
of pie you order in a restaurant on
a country road one cozy evening—the best
piece of pie you have ever eaten in
your life—and can never find again.

~ LEMONY SNICKET

Eden is that old-fashioned house
We dwell in every day
Without suspecting our abode
Until we drive away.

~ EMILY DICKINSON

Maybe that's the best part of going away
for a vacation—coming home again.

~ MADELEINE L'ENGLE
MEET THE AUSTINS

Home is a place you grow up
wanting to leave, and grow old
wanting to get back to.

~ John Ed Pearce

Home is not where you live but
where they understand you.

~ CHRISTIAN MORGENSTERN

AUGUST 31

Peace—that was the
other name for home.

~ KATHLEEN NORRIS

SEPTEMBER

FAITH

Without faith, nothing is possible.
With it, nothing is impossible.

~ MARY MCLEOD BETHUNE

Be like the bird that, passing on her
flight awhile on boughs too slight, feels
them give way beneath her, and yet sings,
knowing that she hath wings.

~ VICTOR HUGO

Faith is not just something
you have, it's something you do.

~ BARACK OBAMA

All you have to do is look straight
and see the road. And when you see it,
don't sit looking at it—walk.

~ AYN RAND
WE THE LIVING

We are made to persist.
That's how we find out who we are.

~ TOBIAS WOLFF

Failure is impossible.

~ SUSAN B. ANTHONY

SEPTEMBER 7

To one who has faith,
no explanation is necessary.
To one without faith, no
explanation is possible.

~ St. Thomas Aquinas

You know, a heart can be broken—
but it keeps on beating, just the same.

~ FANNIE FLAGG
*FRIED GREEN TOMATOES AT
THE WHISTLE STOP CAFE*

Hope is the only bee that makes
honey without flowers.

~ ROBERT INGERSOLL

SEPTEMBER 10

If you hear a voice within
you say "you cannot paint,"
then by all means paint, and
that voice will be silenced.

~ VINCENT VAN GOGH

Fall seven times and stand up eight.

–JAPANESE PROVERB

SEPTEMBER 12

Every strike brings me closer
to the next home run.

–BABE RUTH

There are years that ask
questions and years that answer.

~ ZORA NEALE HURSTON
THEIR EYES WERE WATCHING GOD

SEPTEMBER 14

All endings are also
beginnings,
we just don't know
it at the time.

~ MITCH ALBOM

People who live in difficult
circumstances need to know that
happy endings are possible.

~ SONIA SOTOMAYOR

When we lose one blessing, another is often
most unexpectedly given in its place.

~ C. S. LEWIS

In the kingdom of hope, there is no winter.

~ RUSSIAN PROVERB

I am not afraid of storms for
I am learning how to sail my ship.

~ LOUISA MAY ALCOTT
LITTLE WOMEN

Faith is the centerpiece of a
connected life. It allows us to live
by the grace of invisible strands.

~ TERRY TEMPEST WILLIAMS

When it is dark enough,
you can see the stars.

- CHARLES A. BEARD

Whether you think
you can or you can't—
you're right.

~ HENRY FORD

To have faith
is to have wings.

~ J. M. BARRIE

If we had no winter, the spring would not be so pleasant: If we did not sometimes taste of adversity, prosperity would not be so welcome.

~ ANNE BRADSTREET

Life is a pure flame, and we live
by an invisible sun within us.

~ SIR THOMAS BROWNE

Above all, don't fear difficult moments.
The best comes from them.

~ Rita Levi-Montalcini

The best way out
is always through.

~ ROBERT FROST

To believe in something not yet proved
and to underwrite it with our lives; it is the
only way we can leave the future open.

~ LILLIAN SMITH

Impossible is not a declaration.
It's a dare. Impossible is potential.
Impossible is temporary.
Impossible is nothing.

– MUHAMMAD ALI

The only courage that
matters is the kind that gets you
from one moment to the next.

~ MIGNON MCLAUGHLIN

Life is a shipwreck, but we must not
forget to sing in the lifeboats.

~ VOLTAIRE

OCTOBER

PERSPECTIVE

Oh, how I regret not having worn a bikini for the entire year I was twenty-six. If anyone young is reading this, go, right this minute, put on a bikini, and don't take it off until you're thirty-four.

~ NORA EPHRON

OCTOBER 2

Normal day, let me be aware
of the treasure you are.

~ MARY JEAN IRION

Some people could look
at a mud puddle and see
an ocean with ships.

~ ZORA NEALE HURSTON
THEIR EYES WERE WATCHING GOD

OCTOBER 4

The way I see it, if you want the rainbow,
you gotta put up with the rain.

~ DOLLY PARTON

Age does not protect you from love, but love
to some extent protects you from age.

~ JEANNE MOREAU

There's a bit of magic in everything,
and some loss to even things out.

~ LOU REED

OCTOBER 7

If you look the right way,
you can see that the
whole world is a garden.

~ FRANCES HODGSON BURNETT
THE SECRET GARDEN

OCTOBER 8

Life is beautiful.

~ LEON TROTSKY

You must not pity me because my
sixtieth year finds me still astonished.
To be astonished is one of the surest ways
of not growing old too quickly.

~ COLETTE

To be interested in the changing
seasons is a happier state
of mind than to be hopelessly
in love with spring.

~ GEORGE SANTAYANA

Write it on your heart that every
day is the best day of the year.

–RALPH WALDO EMERSON

Our birthdays are feathers
in the broad wing of time.

~ JEAN PAUL

Do not spoil what you have by
desiring what you have not; but remember
that what you now have was once
among the things only hoped for.

~ EPICURUS

We can choose to hate
the rain or dance in it.

~ JOAN MARQUES

Since we cannot change reality,
let us change the eyes which see reality.

~ NIKOS KAZANTZAKIS
REPORT TO GRECO

When everything seems to be going against
you, remember that the airplane takes off
against the wind, not with it.

–HENRY FORD

When one door of happiness
closes, another opens; but often
we look so long at the closed door
that we do not see the one that
has been opened for us.

~ HELEN KELLER

There are no facts, only interpretations.

~ FRIEDRICH NIETZSCHE

There is nothing either good or
bad, but thinking makes it so.

~ WILLIAM SHAKESPEARE
HAMLET

OCTOBER 20

Life itself is a gift.

~ DAPHNE ROSE KINGMA

OCTOBER 21

A mistake is simply another
way of doing things.

~ E. B. WHITE

The lowest ebb is the turn of the tide.

~ HENRY WADSWORTH LONGFELLOW

OCTOBER 23

One should
absorb the color
of life, but one
should never
remember its details.

~ OSCAR WILDE

It is always the simple that
produces the marvelous.

~ AMELIA BARR

OCTOBER 25

There are always flowers for those
who want to see them.

~ HENRI MATISSE

OCTOBER 26

The greater part of life is sunshine.

–THOMAS JEFFERSON

Everything we hear is an opinion,
not a fact. Everything we see
is a perspective, not the truth.

~ MARCUS AURELIUS

A little perspective,
like a little humor,
goes a long way.

~ ALLEN KLEIN

OCTOBER 29

Be thankful for what you have;
you'll end up having more.

~ OPRAH WINFREY

There is so much in the world for us all
if we only have the eyes to see it.

~ L. M. MONTGOMERY
ANNE OF THE ISLAND

A weed is no more than
a flower in disguise.

-- JAMES RUSSELL LOWELL

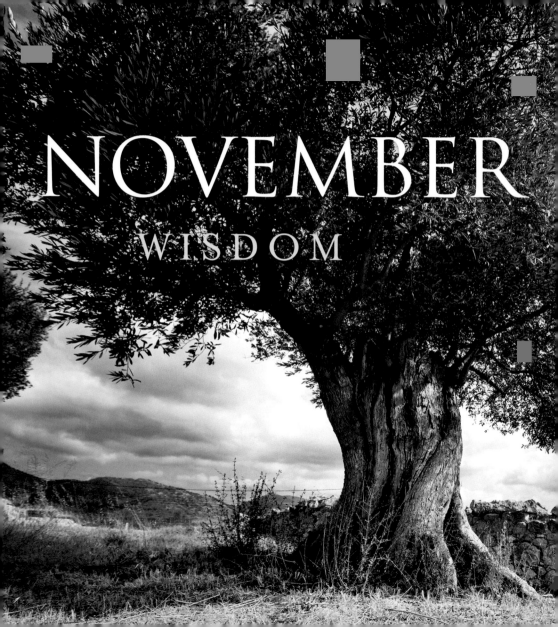

NOVEMBER

WISDOM

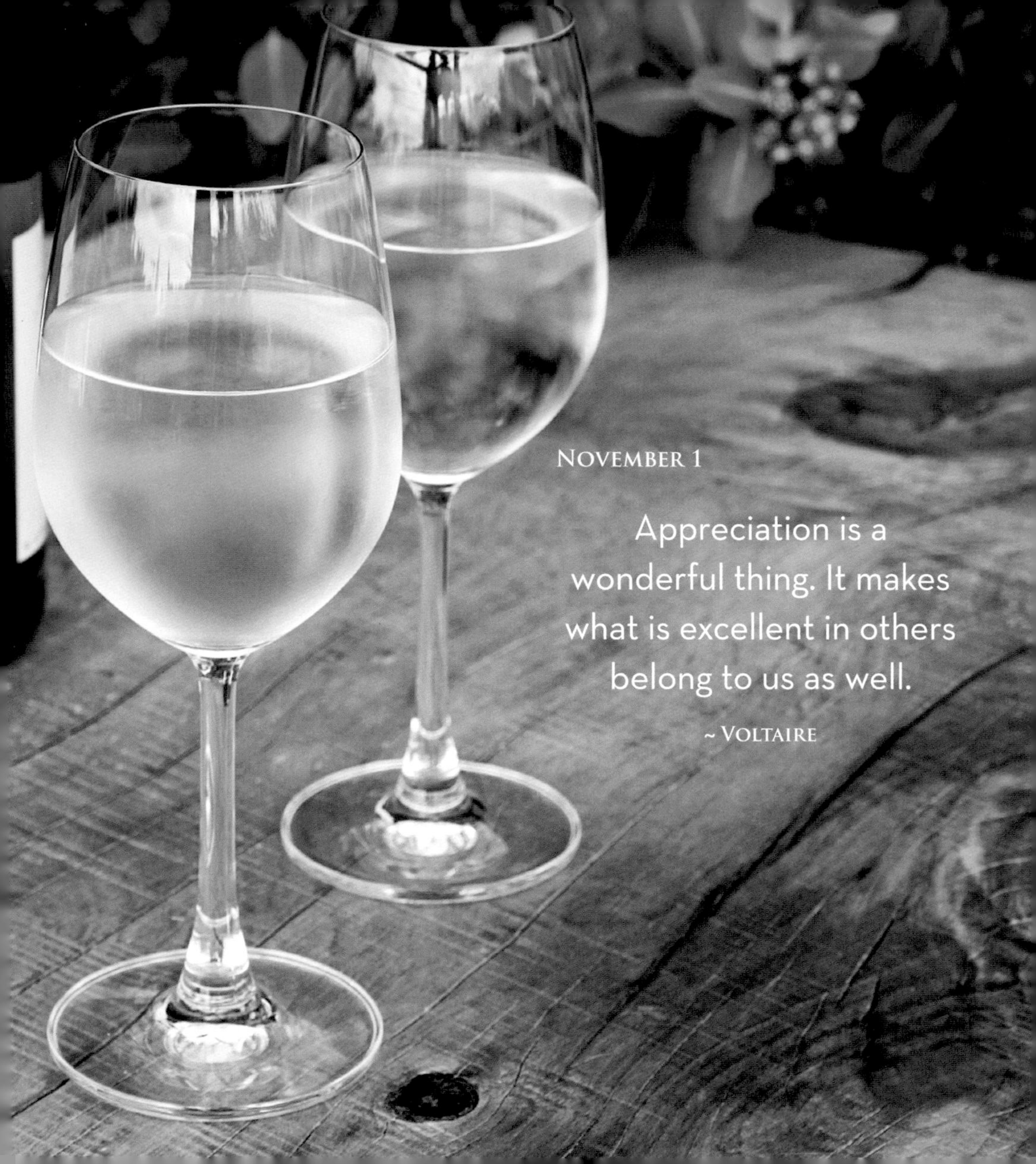

NOVEMBER 1

Appreciation is a wonderful thing. It makes what is excellent in others belong to us as well.

~ VOLTAIRE

A gift is pure when it is given from
the heart to the right person at the right
time and at the right place, and when
we expect nothing in return.

~ VYASA

Integrate what you believe in every single
area of your life. Take your heart to work and
ask the most and best of everybody else too.

~ MERYL STREEP

Time is the coin of your life. It is the
only coin you have, and only you can
determine how it will be spent.

~ CARL SANDBURG

There is no such thing in anyone's
life as an unimportant day.

~ ALEXANDER WOOLLCOTT

The only real elegance
is in the mind; if you've got
that, the rest comes.

~ DIANA VREELAND

How many cares one
loses when one decides
not to be something,
but to be someone.

~ Coco Chanel

Our faces become our biographies.

~ CYNTHIA OZICK

The thing that is really hard,
and really amazing, is giving up
on being perfect and beginning
the work of becoming yourself.

~ ANNA QUINDLEN

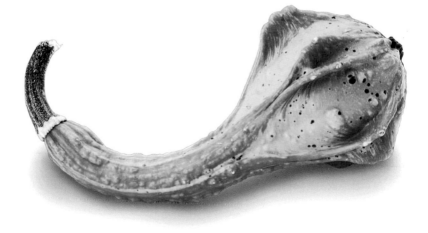

NOVEMBER 10

Our life is the creation of our mind.

~ BUDDHA

They always say that time
changes things, but you actually
have to change them yourself.

~ ANDY WARHOL

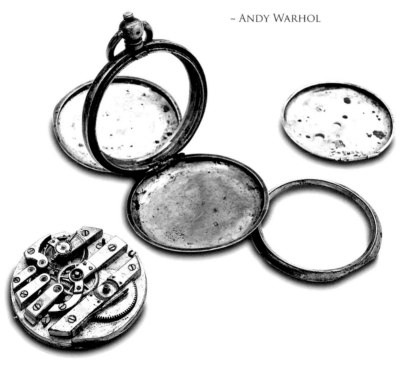

To live is the rarest thing in the world.
Most people exist, that is all.

~ OSCAR WILDE

There is as much greatness of mind in
acknowledging a good turn, as in doing it.

~ SENECA

NOVEMBER 14

Enjoy the little things, for one day you may look
back and realize they were the big things.

~ ROBERT BRAULT

Gratitude is when
memory is stored in the
heart and not in the mind.

~ LIONEL HAMPTON

They who give have all things; they
who withhold have nothing.

~ HINDU PROVERB

Instructions for living a life:
Pay attention. Be astonished. Tell about it.

~ MARY OLIVER

If everyone helps to
hold up the sky, then
one person does not
become tired.

~ TSHI PROVERB

Life shrinks or expands in
proportion to one's courage.

~ ANAÏS NIN

Adopt gratitude as the basic tenor of
one's life—gratitude for being alive, for being
free, healthy, and intelligent; gratitude
for the senses and their pleasures, the mind
and its adventures, the soul and its delights.

~ Johannes A. Gaertner

Life is made up of moments; small pieces of
glittering mica in a long stretch of gray cement.
It would be wonderful if they came
to us unsummoned, but in lives
as busy as the ones most of us lead,
that won't happen. We have to
teach ourselves how to make room for them,
to love them, and to live, really live.

~ ANNA QUINDLEN

Praise the bridge that carried you over.

~ GEORGE COLMAN

NOVEMBER 23

Things do not change;
we change.

~ HENRY DAVID THOREAU

It's never too late—in
fiction or in life—to revise.

~ NANCY THAYER

NOVEMBER 25

Gratitude is one of the
least articulate of
the emotions, especially
when it is deep.

~ FELIX FRANKFURTER

Forget injuries, never forget kindnesses.

~ CONFUCIUS

The purpose of life is to live it, to taste experience to the utmost, to reach out eagerly and without fear for newer and richer experience.

~ ELEANOR ROOSEVELT

Life is ours to be spent, not to be saved.

~ D. H. Lawrence

The greatest thing
in the world is
to know how to belong
to oneself.

~ MICHEL DE MONTAIGNE

NOVEMBER 30

True wisdom lies in
gathering the precious things
out of each hour as it goes by.

~ E. S. BOUTON

DAILY

365 DAYS OF REFLECTION

GRATITUDE

Photos and Wisdom to Enrich Your Spirit

NATIONAL
GEOGRAPHIC

WASHINGTON, D.C.

The National Geographic Society is one of the world's largest nonprofit scientific and
educational organizations. Its mission is to inspire people to care about the planet.
Founded in 1888, the Society is member supported and offers a community for members to
get closer to explorers, connect with other members, and help make a difference. The Society
reaches more than 450 million people worldwide each month through *National Geographic* and
other magazines; National Geographic Channel; television documentaries; music; radio; films;
books; DVDs; maps; exhibitions; live events; school publishing programs; interactive media; and
merchandise. National Geographic has funded more than 10,000 scientific research, conservation,
and exploration projects and supports an education program promoting geographic literacy.
For more information, visit www.nationalgeographic.com.

National Geographic Society
1145 17th Street N.W.
Washington, D.C. 20036-4688 U.S.A.

For information about special discounts for bulk purchases, please contact
National Geographic Books Special Sales: ngspecsales@ngs.org

For rights or permissions inquiries, please contact
National Geographic Books Subsidiary Rights: ngbookrights@ngs.org

Interior design by Marty Ittner

Printed in China

14/PPS/1

JANUARY

GROWTH

Follow your inner moonlight;
don't hide the madness.

~ ALLEN GINSBERG

JANUARY 2

What you have to do is work with
the raw material you have—
namely *you*—and never let up.

~ HELEN GURLEY BROWN

My grandfather once told me that there
were two kinds of people: those who
do the work and those who take the credit.
He told me to try to be in the first group;
there was much less competition.

~ INDIRA GANDHI

To love what you do and
feel it matters—how could
anything be more fun?

~ KATHARINE GRAHAM

Start by doing what's necessary,
then what's possible, and suddenly
you are doing the impossible.

~ ST. FRANCIS OF ASSISI

Tell me, what is it you plan to do
with your one wild and precious life?

~ MARY OLIVER

JANUARY 7

If we don't believe the things we put on
our agendas will come true for us, then
there's no hope for us ... We've got to believe
in our beautiful impossible blueprints.

~ DORIS LESSING
THE GOLDEN NOTEBOOK

If you're offered a seat on a rocket ship,
don't ask what seat! Just get on.

~ SHERYL SANDBERG

You are the one and only ever you.

~ NANCY TILLMAN
ON THE NIGHT YOU WERE BORN

To have that sense of one's intrinsic
worth which constitutes self-respect
is potentially to have everything.

~ JOAN DIDION

Suddenly you find—at age fifty, say—
that a whole new life has opened before
you...as if a fresh sap of ideas
and thoughts was rising in you.

~ AGATHA CHRISTIE

Work while you have the light.
You are responsible for the talent
that has been entrusted to you.

~ HENRI FRÉDÉRIC AMIEL

Start where you are.
Use what you have. Do what you can.

~ ARTHUR ASHE

The privilege of a lifetime
is being who you are.

~ JOSEPH CAMPBELL

JANUARY 15

Somewhere, something
incredible is
waiting to be known.

~ CARL SAGAN

JANUARY 16

Ideas are like rabbits. You get a couple and learn how
to handle them, and pretty soon you have a dozen.

~ JOHN STEINBECK

DECEMBER

HARMONY

DECEMBER 1

Peace cannot be kept by force; it can only be achieved by understanding.

~ ALBERT EINSTEIN

We are happy when for everything inside us
there is a corresponding something outside us.

~ W. B. YEATS

Boredom is the feeling that everything is a
waste of time; serenity, that nothing is.

~ THOMAS SZASZ

DECEMBER 4

Out of clutter, find simplicity.

~ JOHN ARCHIBALD WHEELER

DECEMBER 5

Harmony makes small things grow;
lack of it makes great things decay.

~ SALLUST

Only in peace do we have joy.
Not by acquiring things, not by doing things,
not by earning or learning, but by dedication.

~ SWAMI SATCHIDANANDA

Let things taste
of what they are.

~ ALICE WATERS

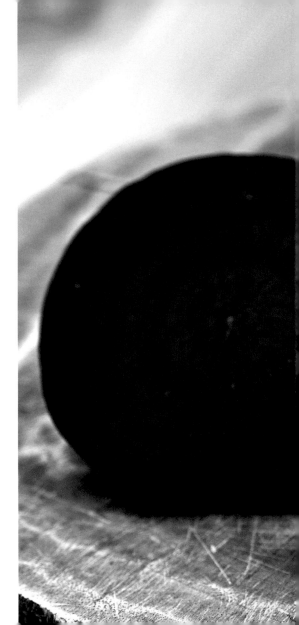

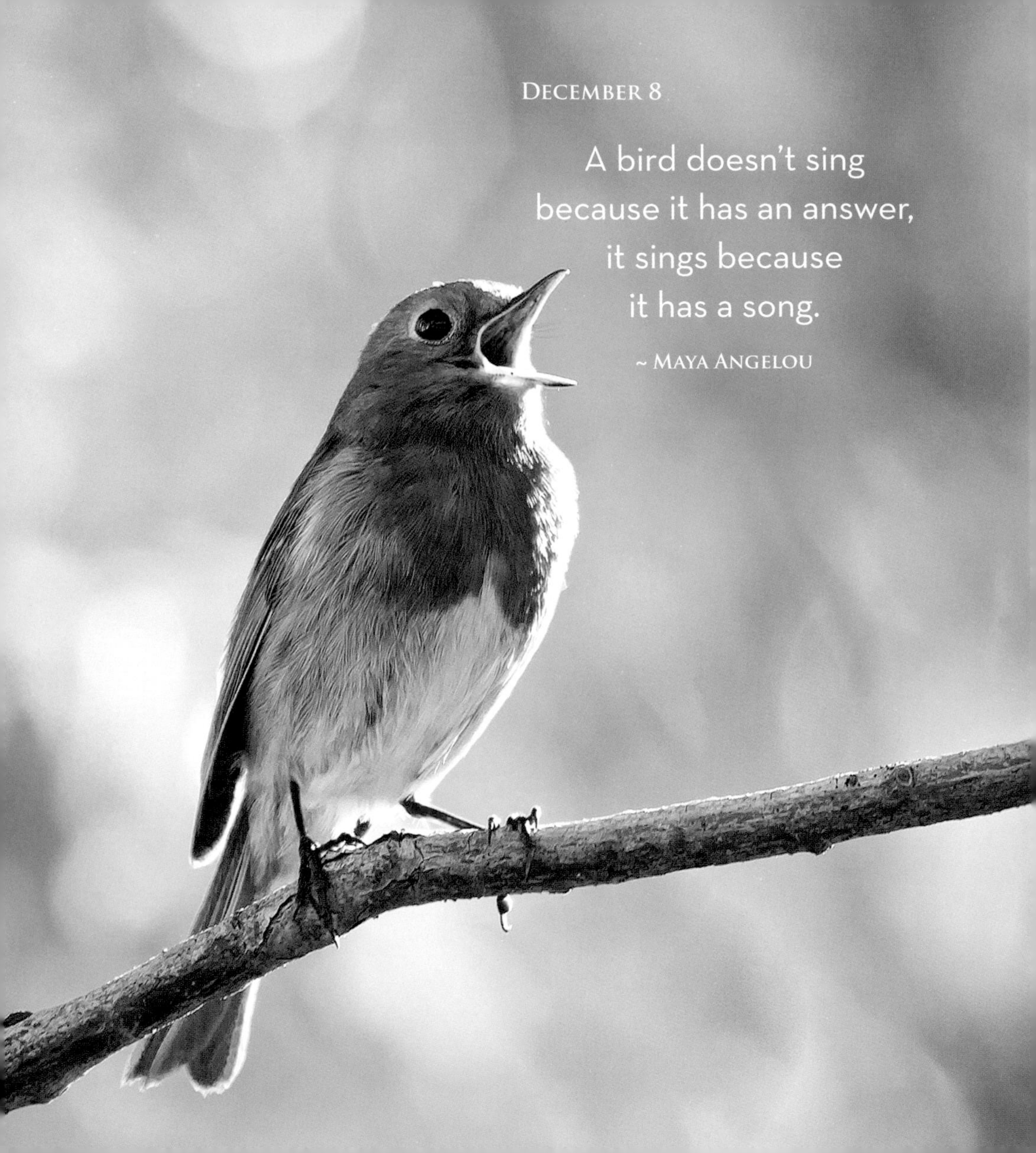

December 8

A bird doesn't sing
because it has an answer,
it sings because
it has a song.

~ Maya Angelou

DECEMBER 9

It is in the shelter of each
other that people live.

~ IRISH PROVERB

DECEMBER 10

After a storm comes a calm.

~ PROVERB

I took a deep breath and listened to the old
brag of my heart. I am. I am. I am.

~ SYLVIA PLATH

There is no greatness where
there is not simplicity.

~ LEO TOLSTOY
WAR AND PEACE

Within you there is a stillness and a sanctuary
to which you can retreat at any time.

~ HERMANN HESSE
SIDDARTHA

DECEMBER 14

The fruit of silence
is tranquility.

~ ARABIAN PROVERB

Watch out for each other. Love everyone and forgive everyone, including yourself. Forgive your anger. Forgive your guilt. Your shame. Your sadness. Embrace and open up your love, your joy, your truth, and most especially your heart.

~ JIM HENSON

Acknowledging the good that you
already have in your life is the
foundation for all abundance.

~ ECKHART TOLLE

The more you lose
yourself in something
bigger than yourself, the
more energy you will have.

~ NORMAN VINCENT PEALE

The way is not in the sky.
The way is in the heart.

~ BUDDHA

There is time
for everything.

~ THOMAS EDISON

It is good to listen—not to voices,
but to the wind blowing, to the brook
running cool over polished stones, to bees
drowsy with the weight of pollen.

~ GLADYS TABER

When you find peace within yourself,
you become the kind of person
who can live at peace with others.

~ PEACE PILGRIM

Cheerfulness keeps up a kind of
daylight in the mind, and fills it with
a steady and perpetual serenity.

~ JOSEPH ADDISON

DECEMBER 23

When you come right
down to it, the secret to
having it all is loving it all.

~ JOYCE BROTHERS

DECEMBER 24

The universe is
made up of stories,
not atoms.

~ MURIEL RUKEYSER

Quiet is peace. Quiet is turning
down the volume knob on life.

~ KHALED HOSSEINI
THE KITE RUNNER

Woke up, it was a
Chelsea morning,
and the first thing
that I knew
There was milk
and toast and honey
and a bowl of
oranges, too.

~ JONI MITCHELL

There are two ways to get enough:
One is to continue to accumulate more
and more. The other is to desire less.

~ G. K. CHESTERTON

The good life is
one inspired by
love and guided
by knowledge.

~ BERTRAND RUSSELL

DECEMBER 29

Darkness cannot drive out darkness:
only light can do that. Hate cannot drive
out hate: only love can do that.

~ MARTIN LUTHER KING, JR.

Like water, we are truest to
our nature in repose.

~ CYRIL CONNOLLY

The first and fundamental
law of nature is to seek out
peace and follow it.

~ THOMAS HOBBES

CREDITS

CONTRIBUTOR INDEX

C

Campbell, Joseph John
1904-1987
American mythologist,
writer, and lecturer.

Capote, Truman
1924-1984
American author.

Carnegie, Dale
1888-1955
American inspirational
author, lecturer, and teacher.

**Carroll, Lewis (Charles
Lutwidge Dodgson)**
1832-1898
English author.

Carson, Rachel
1907-1964
American marine biologist,
writer, and conservationist.

**Carter, Jr., Hodding
William**
1907-1972
American journalist
and author.

Cather, Willa
1873-1947
American author.

Chabon, Michael
b. 1963
American author.

Chanel, Coco (Gabrielle)
1883-1971
French fashion designer.

**Châtelet, Madame
du (Émilie)**
1706-1749
French mathematician,
physicist, and author.

**Chesterton, G. K.
(Gilbert Keith)**
1874-1936
British journalist,
playwright, philosopher,
poet, and critic.

Child, Julia
1912-2004
American chef and
cookbook author.

**Christie, Agatha
(Mary Clarissa)**
1890-1976
English crime writer.

Churchill, Jill
b. 1943
American author.

**Churchill, Winston
Spencer**
1874-1965
British prime minister
and statesman.

Cicero, Marcus Tullius
106-43 B.C.
Roman philosopher,
statesman, and orator.

Coleridge, Samuel Taylor
1772-1834
English poet, literary critic,
and philosopher.

Colette (Sidonie-Gabrielle)
1873-1954
French novelist.

Colman, George
1762-1836
English dramatist.

Colton, Charles Caleb
1780-1832
English clergyman
and writer.

Confucius
551-479 B.C.
Chinese philosopher
and teacher.

Connolly, Cyril
1903-1974
British critic.

Cosby, Bill
b. 1937
American comedian,
actor, and author.

**cummings, e. e.
(Edward Estlin)**
1894-1962
American poet, painter,
essayist, and playwright.

D

Dahl, Roald
1916-1990
British novelist, short-story
writer, and screenwriter.

Dickens, Charles
1812-1870
English writer and
social critic.

Dickinson, Emily
1830-1886
American poet.

Didion, Joan
b. 1934
American journalist
and novelist.

**Dietrich, Marlene
(Marie Magdalene)**
1901-1992
German-born American
actress and singer.

Dillard, Annie
b. 1945
American poet, essayist,
and literary critic.

Dostoyevsky, Fyodor
1821-1881
Russian novelist, short-
story writer, and essayist.

Douglas, Ann
b. 1963
American author.

E

Earhart, Amelia
1897-1937
American aviator.

Edison, Thomas Alva
1847-1931
American inventor and
businessman.

Einstein, Albert
1879-1955
German-American
theoretical physicist.

**Eliot, George (Mary
Ann Evans)**
1819-1880
British novelist.

**Eliot, T. S. (Thomas
Stearns)**
1888-1965
British poet and
playwright.

Emerson, Ralph Waldo
1803-1882
American essayist,
lecturer, and poet.

Ephron, Nora
1941-2012
American screenwriter,
producer, and journalist.

Epicurus
341-269 B.C.
Greek philosopher.

F

Ferguson, Marilyn
1938-2008
American author.

**Fisher, M. F. K. (Mary
Frances Kennedy)**
1908-1992
American food writer.

**Fitzgerald, F. Scott
(Francis Scott Key)**
1896-1940
American author.

Fitzgerald, Zelda
1900-1948
American novelist.

**Flagg, Fannie
(Patricia Neal)**
b. 1944
American author.

Forbes, Malcolm
1919-1990
American businessman
and publisher.

Ford, Henry
1863-1947
American industrialist, inventor, and entrepreneur.

Fox, Michael J.
b. 1961
Canadian-American actor, author, producer, and activist.

Frankfurter, Felix
1882-1965
Associate Justice of the United States Supreme Court.

Freud, Sigmund
1856-1939
Austrian neurologist and father of psychoanalysis.

Fromm, Erich
1900-1980
German-American social psychologist and psychoanalyst.

Frost, Robert
1874-1963
American poet.

G

Gaertner, Johannes (Alexander)
1912-1996
German-American professor, poet, and theologian.

Gandhi, Indira
1917-1984
Indian prime minister and politician.

Gautier, Théophile
1811-1872
French poet, novelist, and journalist.

Gesner, Clark
1938-2002
American composer and songwriter.

Gibran, Kahlil
1883-1931
Lebanese-American artist, poet, writer, and philosopher.

Gilbert, Elizabeth
b. 1969
American writer.

Ginsberg, Allen
1926-1997
American poet.

Giovanni, Nikki (Yolande Cornelia)
b. 1943
American poet.

Goethe, Johann Wolfgang von
1749-1832
German novelist, poet, playwright, and philosopher.

Gogh, Vincent van
1853-1890
Dutch artist.

Goodall, Jane
b. 1934
British primatologist and anthropologist.

Graham, Katharine
1917-2001
American publisher.

Grimes, Martha
b. 1931
American author.

Gunther, John
1901-1970
American journalist and author.

H

Hafez (Shams-ud-din Muhammad)
ca 1320-1389
Persian poet.

Hamilton, Gabrielle
b. 1966
American chef and author.

Hampton, Lionel
1908-2002
American jazz musician.

Hanh, Thich Nhat
b. 1926
Vietnamese Buddhist monk, poet, author, and activist.

Hawking, Stephen
b. 1942
English theoretical physicist, cosmologist, and author.

Hawthorne, Nathaniel
1804-1864
American novelist.

Hemingway, Ernest
1899-1961
American author and journalist.

Henson, Jim
1936-1990
American puppeteer and creator of The Muppets.

Hepburn, Katharine
1907-2003
American actress.

Hesse, Hermann
1877-1962
German-Swiss poet, novelist, and painter.

Hobbes, Thomas
1588-1679
English philosopher.

Holmes, Oliver Wendell, Sr.
1809-1894
American physician, professor, and author.

Horace (Quintus Horatius Flaccus)
65-27 B.C.
Roman lyric poet.

Hosseini, Khaled
b. 1965
Afghan-born American novelist and physician.

Howard, Jane
1935-1996
American journalist.

Hughes, Langston
1902-1967
American poet, novelist, and playwright.

Hughes, Ted
1930-1998
English poet.

Hugo, Victor
1802-1885
French poet, novelist, and dramatist.

Hunt, Leigh (James Henry)
1784-1859
English writer.

Hurston, Zora Neale
1891-1960
American novelist, essayist, and folklorist.

I

Ingersoll, Robert Green
1833-1899
American politician and orator.

Irion, Mary Jean
b. 1922
American writer.

J

Jefferson, Thomas
1743-1826
American President.

Jewett, Sarah Orne
1849-1909
American novelist and short-story writer.

Johnson, Samuel
1709-1784
British poet, essayist, literary critic, and lexicographer.

Jong, Erica
b. 1942
American novelist.

July, Miranda
b. 1974
American filmmaker, actress, and author.

Karr, Jean-Baptiste Alphonse
1808–1890
French journalist, critic, and novelist.

Kassia
ca A.D. 810–ca 865
Byzantine abbess, poet, and composer.

Kazantzakis, Nikos
1883–1957
Greek novelist and philosopher.

Keats, John
1795–1821
British poet.

Keller, Helen
1880–1968
American writer, lecturer, and activist.

Kent, Sister Corita (Frances Elizabeth)
1918–1986
American artist and educator.

Kidd, Sue Monk
b. 1948
American writer.

Kimbrough, Emily
1899–1989
American author and journalist.

King, Martin Luther, Jr.
1929–1968
American clergyman, activist, and leader.

Kingma, Daphne Rose
b. 1942
American writer and therapist.

Kingsolver, Barbara
b. 1955
American novelist, poet, and essayist.

Klein, Allen
1931–2009
American businessman.

Lamott, Anne
b. 1954
American novelist and nonfiction writer.

Lawrence, D. H. (David Herbert)
1885–1930
English novelist.

L'Engle, Madeleine
1918–2007
American writer.

Lessing, Doris
1919–2013
British novelist and poet.

Levi-Montalcini, Rita
1909–2012
Italian neurologist.

Lewis, C. S. (Clive Staples)
1898–1963
Irish novelist, scholar, and broadcaster.

Lin Yutang
1895–1976
Chinese novelist, essayist, and translator.

Lindbergh, Anne Morrow
1906–2001
American writer, poet, and aviator.

Longfellow, Henry Wadsworth
1807–1882
American poet.

Lowell, James Russell
1819–1891
American poet.

Mandela, Nelson
1918–2013
South African President.

Marques, Joan
b. 1960
South American professor and writer.

Matisse, Henri (Émile-Benoît)
1869–1954
French artist.

Maurois, André
1885–1967
French biographer, novelist, and essayist.

McCandless, Christopher Johnson (Alexander Supertramp)
1968–1992
American adventurer.

McCarthy, Cormac
b. 1933
American novelist.

McCarthy, Mary
1912–1989
American author.

McLaughlin, Mignon
1913–1983
American journalist and writer.

Meltzer, Bernard
1916–1998
American radio personality.

Mitchell, Joni
b. 1943
Canadian musician and painter.

Montaigne, Michel de
1533–1592
French writer and philosopher.

Montgomery, L. M. (Lucy Maud)
1874–1942
Canadian novelist.

Moore, Thomas
1779–1852
Irish poet.

Moreau, Jeanne
b. 1928
French actress.

Morgenstern, Christian
1871–1914
German author and poet.

Morrison, Toni (Chloe Ardelia Wofford)
b. 1931
American novelist and poet.

Muir, John
1838–1914
Scottish-American naturalist, author, and activist.

Munro, Alice
b. 1931
Canadian author.

Murakami, Haruki
b. 1949
Japanese writer.

Murdoch, Iris
1919–1999
British novelist and philosopher.

Neruda, Pablo
1904–1973
Chilean poet, diplomat, and politician.

Nietzsche, Friedrich
1844–1900
German philosopher and poet.

Nin, Anaïs
1903–1977
French diarist and novelist.

Norris, Kathleen
b. 1947
American poet and essayist.

O

Oates, Joyce Carol
b. 1938
American author.

Obama, Barack Hussein
b. 1961
American President.

O'Keeffe, Georgia
1887–1986
American artist.

Oliver, Mary
b. 1935
American poet.

Orlean, Susan
b. 1955
American journalist
and author.

O'Rourke, Meghan
b. 1976
American essayist
and poet.

Ozick, Cynthia
b. 1928
American novelist
and essayist.

P

Palahniuk, Chuck
b. 1962
American novelist.

Parker, Dorothy
1893–1967
American satirist, critic,
and poet.

Parton, Dolly
b. 1946
American singer-songwriter.

**Paul, Jean (Johann Paul
Friedrich Richter)**
1763–1825
German writer.

Peale, Norman Vincent
1898–1993
American author and
minister.

Pearce, John Ed
1917–2006
American journalist.

**Pilgrim, Peace
(Mildred Norman Ryder)**
1908–1981
American pacifist and
activist.

Plath, Sylvia
1932–1963
American poet, novelist,
and short-story writer.

Proust, Marcel
1871–1922
French novelist.

Q

Quindlen, Anna
b. 1953
American journalist
and novelist.

R

Rand, Ayn
1905–1982
American novelist.

Reed, Lou (Lewis Allan)
1942–2013
American musician.

Reichl, Ruth
b. 1948
American food writer.

Roosevelt, (Anna) Eleanor
1884–1962
American First Lady,
activist, and author.

Rossetti, Christina
1830–1894
English poet.

Rowland, Helen
1875–1950
American journalist.

Rukeyser, Muriel
1913–1980
American poet and
political activist.

**Rumi (Jalal ad-Din
ar-Rumi)**
1207–1273
Persian poet.

Ruskin, John
1819–1900
British art critic and
philanthropist.

Russell, Bertrand
1872–1970
British philosopher,
mathematician, and
social critic.

**Ruth, Babe
(George Herman)**
1895–1948
American baseball player.

S

Sagan, Carl
1934–1996
American astronomer,
astrophysicist, and author.

**Sallust
(Gaius Crispus Sallustius)**
86–35 B.C.
Roman historian.

Sandberg, Sheryl
b. 1969
American businesswoman.

Sandburg, Carl
1878–1967
American writer and poet.

Sandmaier, Marian
b. 1948
American writer
and book editor.

Santayana, George
1863–1952
Spanish-American philo-
sopher, poet, and novelist.

**Satchidananda, Swami (C.
K. Ramaswamy Gounder)**
1914–2002
Indian religious teacher.

Schmich, Mary
b. 1953
American columnist.

Schweitzer, Albert
1875–1965
German and French
philosopher, musician,
and physician.

**Seneca, Lucius Annaeus
(Seneca the Younger)**
4 B.C.,–A.D. 65
Roman philosopher,
statesman, and dramatist.

Shakespeare, William
1564–1616
British playwright and poet.

Smith, Lillian
1897–1966
American writer.

**Snicket, Lemony
(Daniel Handler)**
b. 1970
American author.

Sotomayor, Sonia
b. 1954
American Supreme
Court Justice.

Steinbeck, John
1902–1968
American novelist

Stevenson, Robert Louis
1850–1894
Scottish novelist, poet,
and writer.

Stone, Elizabeth
b. 1959
American professor,
journalist, and author.

Stoppard, Tom
b. 1937
British playwright and
screenwriter.

Stowe, Harriet Beecher
1811–1896
American abolitionist
and author.

Strayed, Cheryl
b. 1968
American memoirist,
novelist, and columnist.

Streep, Meryl
b. 1949
American actress.

Szasz, Thomas
1920–2012
American psychiatrist
and professor.

T

Taber, Gladys
1899–1980
American author and
professor.

Taupin, Bernie
b. 1950
English lyricist, poet,
and singer.

**Teresa, Mother (Agnes
Gonxha Bojaxhiu)**
1910–1997
Albanian-Indian nun
and religious leader.

Thayer, Nancy
b. 1943
American author.

Thoreau, Henry David
1817–1862
American author, poet,
and philosopher.

Thucydides
ca 460–ca 395 B.C.
Greek historian and
Athenian general.

Tillman, Nancy
b. 1955
American author of
children's books.

**Tolkien, J. R. R. (John
Ronald Reuel)**
1892–1973
English writer, poet,
and professor.

Tolle, Eckhart
b. 1948
German spiritual teacher
and writer.

Tolstoy, Leo
1828–1910
Russian novelist and
short-story writer.

Traherne, Thomas
1636–1674
English poet and
theologian.

Trotsky, Leon
1879–1940
Russian revolutionary.

Tutu, Desmond
b. 1931
South African religious leader
and antiapartheid activist.

**Twain, Mark (Samuel
Langhorne Clemens)**
1835–1910
American novelist and
humorist.

Tyger, Frank
1929–2011
American cartoonist,
columnist, and humorist.

V

van Dyke, Henry
1852–1933
American author, educator,
and clergyman.

**Voltaire (François-Marie
Arouet)**
1694–1778
French writer, playwright,
and philosopher

Vreeland, Diana
1903–1989
American editor.

Vyasa
ca 3000 B.C.
Hindu spiritual leader.

W

Walker, Alice
b. 1944
American novelist, poet,
and activist.

Walls, Jeannette
b. 1960
American writer and
journalist.

Warhol, Andy
1928–1987
American artist.

Waters, Alice
b. 1944
American chef, activist,
and author.

Webster, Jean
1876–1916
American author.

Welty, Eudora
1909–2001
American author.

West, Mae (Mary Jane)
1893–1980
American actress,
playwright, and
screenwriter.

**Wharton, Edith
(Newbold Jones)**
1862–1937
American novelist.

Wheeler, John Archibald
1911–2008
American theoretical
physicist.

**White, E. B. (Elwyn
Brooks)**
1899–1985
American writer.

Wilcox, Ella Wheeler
1850–1919
American author and poet.

Wilde, Oscar
1854–1900
Irish novelist and dramatist.

Wilder, Laura Ingalls
1867–1957
American author.

Wilder, Thornton
1897–1975
American playwright
and novelist.

**Williams, Tennessee
(Thomas Lanier)**
1911–1983
American playwright,
novelist, and essayist.

**Williams, Terry
Tempest**
b. 1955
American author
and activist.

**Williams, William
Carlos**
1883–1963
American poet.

Wilson, Woodrow
1856–1924
American President.

Winfrey, Oprah
b. 1954
American media personality.

Wolff, Tobias
b. 1945
American author.

Woodward, Joanne
b. 1930
American actress and
producer.

Woolf, Virginia (Adeline)
1882–1941
British novelist and
essayist.

Woollcott, Alexander
1887–1943
American playwright and
drama critic.

Wordsworth, William
1770–1850
English poet.

Wright, Frank Lloyd
1867–1959
American architect.

Y

**Yeats, W. B.
(William Butler)**
1865–1939
Irish poet.

ILLUSTRATIONS CREDITS

Blazej Lyjak/Shutterstock; 12, Blaz Kure/Shutterstock; 13, Arman Zhenikeyev/Corbis; 14, Floortje/iStockphoto; 15, lambada/iStockphoto; 16, Arne Bramsen/Shutterstock; 17, wavebreakmedia/Shutterstock; 18, deadplant155/iStockphoto; 19, Jostaphot/iStockphoto; 20, Chris Johns/National Geographic Creative; 21, 2009fotofriends/Shutterstock; 22, icyimage/iStockphoto; 23, Keren Su/Corbis; 24, jeep2499/Shutterstock; 25, LynneAlbright/iStockphoto; 26, MarclSchauer/Shutterstock; 27, Michael Nichols/National Geographic Creative; 28, Volkmar Wentzel/National Geographic Creative; 29, Bruce Dale/National Geographic Creative; 30, Royalty Free Stock Photos/Shutterstock.

MAY

Opener, Calek/Shutterstock; 1, Krisdayod/Shutterstock; 2, ApoXX/iStockphoto; 3, PlusONE/Shutterstock; 4, serezniy/iStockphoto; 5, KeenPress/National Geographic Creative; 6, Givaga/Shutterstock; 7, Racide/iStockphoto; 8, Irina Mosina/Shutterstock; 9, Tetra Images/Getty Images; 10, MARGRIT HIRSCH/Shutterstock; 11, Butterfly Hunter/Shutterstock; 12, Algefoto/Shutterstock; 13, MoreISO/iStockphoto; 14, Narong Jongsirikul/Shutterstock; 15, Catherine Karnow/National Geographic Creative; 16, DIOMEDIA/Alamy; 17, MarkMirror/Shutterstock; 18, blickwinkel/Alamy; 19, Maravic/iStockphoto; 20, Roman Striga/Shutterstock; 21, ilolab/Shutterstock; 22, Grisha Bruev/Shutterstock; 23, Alex Emanuel Koch/Shutterstock; 24, Julie Boro/Shutterstock; 25, ponsulak/Shutterstock; 26, BasPhoto/iStockphoto; 27, Peter Wey/Shutterstock; 28, Aigars Jukna/Shutterstock; 29, Peeter Viisimaa/iStockphoto; 30, Firmston, Victoria/the food passionates/Corbis; 31, Dinesh Hegde/National Geographic Your Shot.

JUNE

Opener, Phil Schermeister; 1, Becky Stares/Shutterstock; 2, 4allthingsweb/iStockphoto; 3, Jerzy Bin/Shutterstock; 4, Paul Prescott/Shutterstock; 5, Boyd Hendrikse/Shutterstock; 6, Darlyne A. Murawski/National Geographic Creative; 7, Thomas J. Abercrombie/National Geographic Creative; 8, Grisha Bruev/Shutterstock; 9, Iakov Kalinin/Shutterstock; 10, Konrad Wothe/Minden Pictures/National Geographic Creative; 11, Konstanttin/Shutterstock; 12, Jim Brandenburg/National Geographic Creative; 13, SusaZoom/Shutterstock; 14, Stewart Smith Photography/Shutterstock; 15, Robbie George/National Geographic Creative; 16, Draw05/Shutterstock; 17, YuryZap/

Shutterstock; 18, Anna Chelnokova/Shutterstock; 19, WhiteTag/Shutterstock; 20, Amy White & Al Petteway/National Geographic Creative; 21, George Dolgikh/Shutterstock; 22, Chris Pritchard/iStockphoto; 23, Suzanne Stevenson/Shutterstock; 24, MichaelUtech/iStockphoto; 25, Jodi Cobb/National Geographic Creative; 26, MikeLaptev/iStockphoto; 27, Aziz Dhamani/National Geographic Your Shot; 28, PaulTessier/iStockphoto; 29, peter zelei/iStockphoto; 30, Raymond Gehman/National Geographic Creative.

JULY

Opener, Shaiith/Dreamstime.com; 1, HENX/Shutterstock; 2, Willyam Bradberry/Shutterstock; 3, Phil Schermeister; 4, Juanmonino/iStockphoto; 5, Buzz Productions/iStockphoto; 6, Scott Sroka/National Geographic Creative; 7, wassiliy-architect/Shutterstock; 8, Luis Marden/National Geographic Creative; 9, wragg/iStockphoto; 10, peter zelei/iStockphoto; 11, Chris Hill/National Geographic Creative; 12, Elias Kordelakos/Shutterstock; 13, Pictureguy/Shutterstock; 14, Ron and Patty Thomas Photography/iStockphoto; 15, Annie Griffiths/National Geographic Creative; 16, Maria Stenzel/National Geographic Creative; 17, George Steinmetz; 18, Sara Winter/iStockphoto; 19, Maglara/Shutterstock; 20, tr3gi/iStockphoto; 21, Demansia/iStockphoto; 22, Fabian Wentzel/iStockphoto; 23, Paul Reeves Photography/Shutterstock; 24, Julia Sumerling/National Geographic Your Shot; 25, ballycroy/iStockphoto; 26, Terry Wilson/iStockphoto; 27, Mike Tauber/Blend Images/Corbis; 28, Diane Cook & Len Jenshel/National Geographic Creative; 29, Anna Morgan/Shutterstock; 30, Joel Sartore/National Geographic Creative; 31, Carsten Peter/National Geographic Creative.

AUGUST

Opener, Terrie L. Zeller/Shutterstock; 1, felinda/iStockphoto; 2, Catherine Karnow/National Geographic Creative; 3, nicolas_/iStockphoto; 4, Kletr/Shutterstock; 5, Maglara/Shutterstock; 6, Antonov Roman/Shutterstock; 7, bikeriderlondon/Shutterstock; 8, Artens/Shutterstock; 9, SusaZoom/Shutterstock; 10, Meowgli/iStockphoto; 11, James P. Blair/National Geographic Stock; 12, tiler84/iStockphoto; 13, mubus7/Shutterstock; 14, James P. Blair/National Geographic Creative; 15, Jaromir Chalabala/Shutterstock; 16, Trybex/Shutterstock; 17, ThomasVogel/iStockphoto; 18,

Helen Filatova/Shutterstock; 19, Lisa A/Shutterstock; 20, Elena Schweitzer/Shutterstock; 21, fotolinchen/iStockphoto; 22, compassandcamera/iStockphoto; 23, Jens Ottoson/Shutterstock; 24, Ocean/Corbis; 25, Jacynthroode/iStockphoto; 26, Peter O'Toole/Shutterstock; 27, Steve Buckley/Shutterstock; 28, Fingerszz/iStockphoto; 29, Michael Shake/Shutterstock; 30, zofia/iStockphoto; 31, George F. Mobley/National Geographic Creative.

SEPTEMBER

Opener, Rrrainbow/iStockphoto; 1, isa3863/iStockphoto; 2, sdbower/iStockphoto; 3, Yva Momatiuk & John Eastcott/Minden Pictures/Corbis; 4, Dave Allen Photography/Shutterstock; 5, Yuri Yavnik/Shutterstock; 6, Jitchanamont/Shutterstock; 7, YinYang/iStockphoto; 8, Maxim Tupikov/Shutterstock; 9, StudioSmart/Shutterstock; 10, Nudda Chollamark/123rf.com; 11, Justinreznick/iStockphoto; 12, Mark Thiessen/National Geographic Creative; 13, Xico Putini/Shutterstock; 14, Amy White & Al Petteway/National Geographic Creative; 15, Pecold/Shutterstock; 16, Ying Feng Johansson/Dreamstime.com; 17, Gti861/iStockphoto; 18, Mihej/iStockphoto; 19, Simona Dumitru/123rf.com; 20, stmeca/iStockphoto; 21, Macduff Everton/National Geographic Creative; 22, Frank Leung/iStockphoto; 23, Weerachai Khamfu/Shutterstock; 24, mukesh-kumar/iStockphoto; 25, Maridav/Shutterstock; 26, GiorgioMagini/iStockphoto; 27, nick82p/iStockphoto; 28, Linda Steward/iStockphoto; 29, Neale Cousland/Shutterstock; 30, Iakov Kalinin/Shutterstock.

OCTOBER

Opener, Piyapunt Paetanom/123RF; 1, Mike Flippo/Shutterstock; 2, StephanieFrey/iStockphoto; 3, Luis Marden/National Geographic Creative; 4, TTstudio/Shutterstock; 5, Byron Yu/National Geographic Your Shot; 6, Shin Yoshino/Minden Pictures/National Geographic Creative; 7, 1Photodiva/iStockphoto; 8, Steve Winter; 9, mariobono/iStockphoto; 10, mashabuba/iStockphoto; 11, deepblue4you/iStockphoto; 12, Prill Medendesign & Fotografie/iStockphoto; 13, gdvcom/Shutterstock; 14, ozgurdonmaz/iStockphoto; 15, Kokhanchikov/Shutterstock; 16, Jeff Mauritzen/National Geographic Creative; 17, Tacit/cultura/Corbis; 18, V. Kuntsman/Shutterstock; 19, Wiktory/iStockphoto; 20, Mint Images/Art Wolfe/Getty Images; 21, Eduard Andras/iStockphoto; 22, haveseen/Shutterstock; 23, Neale Cousland/Shutterstock; 24, RJ Grant/Shutterstock;

25, Maartje van Caspel/iStockphoto; 26, Stephen Cockley/National Geographic Your Shot; 27, Mike Liu/Shutterstock; 28, Robert B. Haas; 29, Alejandro Rivera/iStockphoto; 30, redmal/iStockphoto; 31, bgwalker/iStockphoto.

NOVEMBER

Opener, FredFroese/iStockphoto; 1, Pixsooz/iStockphoto; 2, Kaspars Grinvalds/Shutterstock; 3, gualtiero boffi/Shutterstock; 4, maigi/Shutterstock; 5, Gord Horne/iStockphoto; 6, bisla/iStockphoto; 7, Amy White & Al Petteway/National Geographic Creative; 8, Michael Nichols/National Geographic Creative; 9, Cousin_Avi/Shutterstock; 10, Voranat Rajchatan/123RF; 11, Sergej Razvodovskij/Shutterstock; 12, Ammit Jack/Shutterstock; 13, Anna_Pustynnikova/Shutterstock; 14, Yuri_Arcurs/iStockphoto; 15, Evgeniya Uvarova/Shutterstock; 16, Rebecca Hale/National Geographic Creative; 17, ideabug/iStockphoto; 18, tschuma417/iStockphoto; 19, kenneth-cheung/iStockphoto; 20, vvvita/Shutterstock; 21, Victor R. Boswell, Jr./National Geographic Creative; 22, JPL Designs/Shutterstock; 23, Frans Lanting/National Geographic Creative; 24, Sam Abell/National Geographic Creative; 25, Brian Skerry/National Geographic Creative; 26, mikedabell/iStockphoto; 27, James L. Stanfield/National Geographic Creative; 28, Triff/Shutterstock; 29, nehru/123RF; 30, angelakatharina/Shutterstock.

DECEMBER

Opener, Estea/Shutterstock; 1, 123stocks/iStockphoto; 2, EMprize/Shutterstock; 3, Sergieiev/Shutterstock.com; 4, Stokkete/Shutterstock; 5, AXL/Shutterstock; 6, maximkabb/iStockphoto; 7, Amy Le/Shutterstock; 8, Tadas_Naujokaitis/Shutterstock; 9, Chris Hill/National Geographic Creative; 10, Matt Gibson/Shutterstock; 11, Ronald Sumners/Shutterstock; 12, Arunas Gabalis/Shutterstock; 13, t_kimura/iStockphoto; 14, esolla/iStockphoto; 15, Darlyne A. Murawski/National Geographic Creative; 16, Jimmy Tran/Shutterstock; 17, Kate Thompson/National Geographic Creative; 18, MO_SES Premium/Shutterstock; 19, Tischenko Irina/Shutterstock; 20, Phil Schermeister; 21, Anna Omelchenko/iStockphoto; 22, Anna-Mari West/Shutterstock; 23, amenic181/Shutterstock; 24, Chintla/Shutterstock; 25, stoonn/Shutterstock; 26, Philary/iStockphoto; 27, alantobey/iStockphoto; 28, Maglara/Shutterstock; 29, Wanchai Orsuk/Shutterstock; 30, diephosi/iStockphoto; 31, Jerzy Bin/National Geographic Your Shot.

Daily Gratitude

Published by the National Geographic Society

Gary E. Knell, *President and Chief Executive Officer*

John M. Fahey, *Chairman of the Board*

Declan Moore, *Executive Vice President; President, Publishing and Travel*

Melina Gerosa Bellows, *Executive Vice President; Publisher and Chief Creative Officer, Books, Kids, and Family*

Prepared by the Book Division

Hector Sierra, *Senior Vice President and General Manager*

Janet Goldstein, *Senior Vice President and Editorial Director*

Jonathan Halling, *Creative Director*

Marianne R. Koszorus, *Design Director*

Hilary Black, *Senior Editor*

R. Gary Colbert, *Production Director*

Jennifer A. Thornton, *Director of Managing Editorial*

Susan S. Blair, *Director of Photography*

Meredith C. Wilcox, *Director, Administration and Rights Clearance*

Staff for This Book

Melissa Farris, *Art Director*

Nancy Marion, *Illustrations Editor*

Marty Ittner, *Designer*

Anne Smyth, *Assistant Editor*

Marnie Hanel, *Researcher*

Kristina Heitkamp, *Assistant Researcher*

Marshall Kiker, *Associate Managing Editor*

Judith Klein, *Production Editor*

Lisa A. Walker, *Production Manager*

Galen Young, *Rights Clearance Specialist*

Katie Olsen, *Production Design Assistant*

Production Services

Phillip L. Schlosser, *Senior Vice President*

Chris Brown, *Vice President, NG Book Manufacturing*

Nicole Elliott, *Director of Production*

George Bounelis, *Senior Production Manager*

Rachel Faulise, *Manager*

Robert L. Barr, *Manager*